3

Merida's Home
from Disney-Pixar's Brave

Intermediate Harp Version

Music by Patrick Doyle
Harp arrangement by Sylvia Woods

Quickly

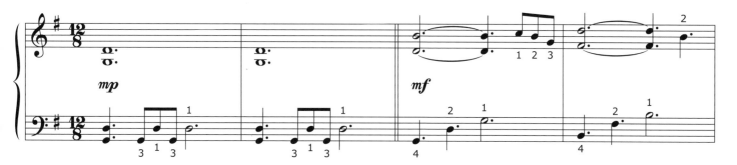

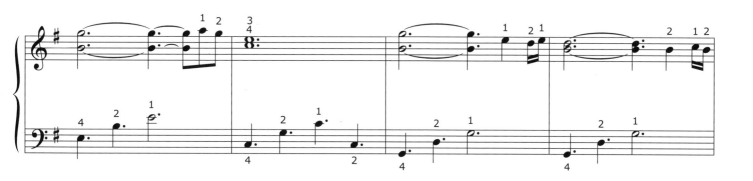

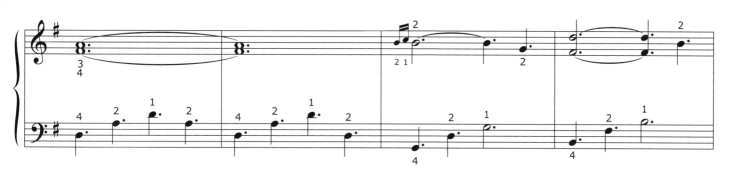

5

Noble Maiden Fair
(A Mhaighdean Bhan Uasal)
from Disney-Pixar's <u>Brave</u>

The Gaelic lyrics are the top line, with a phonetic version below.

Music by Patrick Doyle
Lyrics by Patrick Neil Doyle
Harp arrangement by Sylvia Woods

Slowly, as a lullaby ♩=126

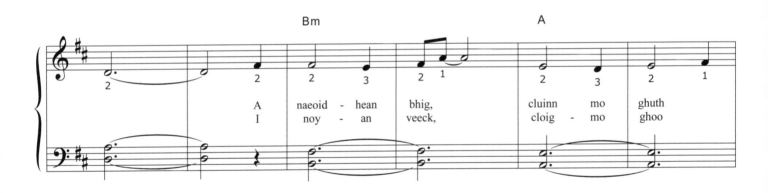

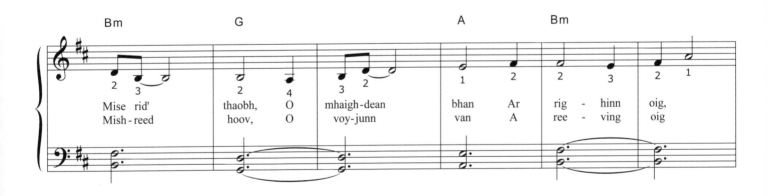

8

9

Learn Me Right
from Disney-Pixar's Brave

Words and Music by Marcus Mumford
Winston Marshall, Ted Dwane and Ben Lovett
Harp arrangement by Sylvia Woods

Moderate Folk Waltz

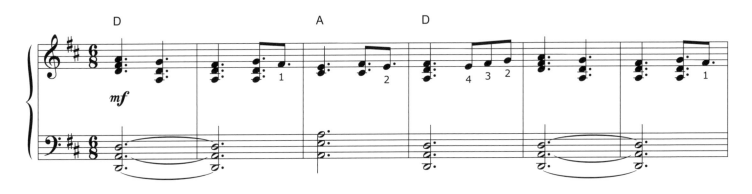

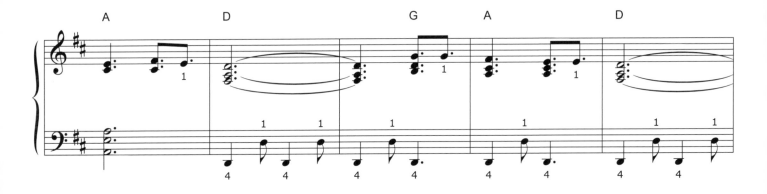

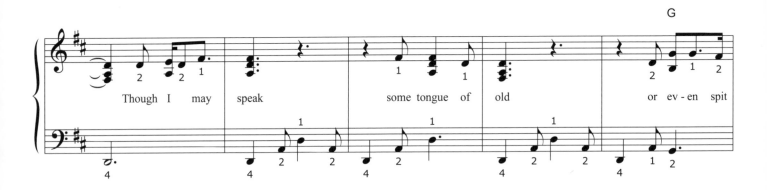

Though I may speak some tongue of old or ev-en spit

13

Into the Open Air
from Disney-Pixar's <u>Brave</u>

Words and Music by Alexander L. Mandel
Harp arrangement by Sylvia Woods

18

And now these walls come crum - bl - ing down?

And I can feel my feet on the ground.

Can we car - ry this love that we share. In -

to the op - - en air.

This love it is a burn - ing sun.

rit.

The Games
from Disney-Pixar's Brave

Music by Patrick Doyle
Harp arrangement by Sylvia Woods

Lever harp players: All C strings should be set to C natural.

Touch the Sky
from Disney-Pixar's Brave

Music by Alexander L. Mandel
Lyrics by Alexander L. Mandel
and Mark Andrews
Harp arrangement by Sylvia Woods

Lever harp players: set all Cs to C natural.
Set the F below middle C to an F natural

Quickly

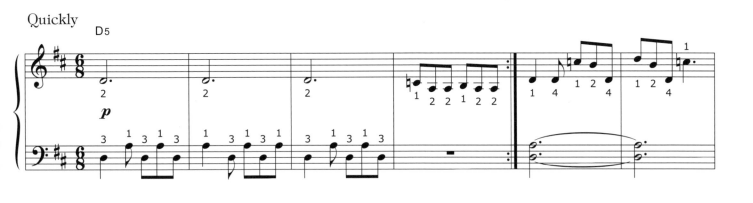

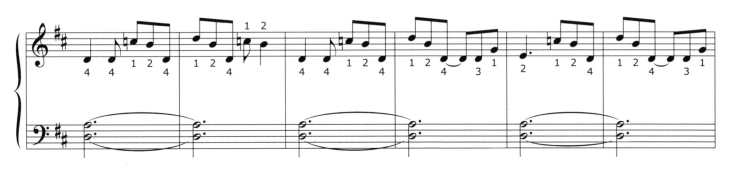

23